"I can't think of a gr
ing to the Lord and
will be blessed as you ʀᴇᴀᴅ

Bishop G.J. & Carla Chandler, ᴇᴠᴀɴɢᴇ...
Cullman, AL

"Incredible story! What an amazing God we serve! Your testimony will be a blessing and bring hope to a lot of people in so many ways!"

Bishop Ron & Coleen Stewart, Senior Pastors
Abundant Life Church of God
Lakeland, FL

"A beautiful testimony of the love of both an earthly father and our heavenly Father!"

Pastor Justin & Jaime Stewart
Mission Florida
Abundant Life Church of God
Lakeland, FL

"If you need to know God's awesome love then this book is for you. Don't give up on God! God is and God will show His love."

Pastor Ed & Carla Chandler
Durand Church of God
Durand, MI

"A modern day version of the Prodigal Son. A son with feelings of being a failure, returns home to discover his father's love was never based on his performance. This is a true testimony of the power of unconditional love."

Bishop Jerry & Darla Shepherd
20th Avenue Church of God
Vero Beach, FL

"This Incredible Story will show you God's Amazing Power of Love, Salvation, Miracles, Healing and Restoration of Life! It is an Anointed and Inspirational Truth of how God moves in the lives of those that will surrender to Him! If God can do it for this Family He can and will do it for you and your Family! We strongly recommend it to all who want to make a difference for the Kingdom of God and in the lives of their families!"

Bishop Troy & Denise Puckett, Senior Pastors
Simcoe Worship Center Church of God
Cullman, Alabama

If you like reading life stories, you will love this one! Many of life's problematic situations are part of this story. Frustration, rebellion, blaming oneself, anger, spirituality, etc., etc., to name a few - I'll not list all of them because I do not want to give away the story. You'll find many of the problems that you deal with somewhere in this book.

You will also find "solutions" to life's problem's in this book. Sacrifice, love, forgiveness, renewed relationships, Godliness, to name a few!

If you are dealing with family or spiritual issues, you must read this book. What better way can we learn to deal with situations in our life than seeing how other's deal with similar issue's. I know the people who give us this story. The story is accurate and given for the purpose of helping others. Now, several years after the events of the book, their lives' are still changed. Real solutions bring real change. If you need a "real change", let this book speak to you.

Bishop Larry J. Anderson
Pastor at Victorious Life Church
Ypsilanti, Michigan

THE FATHER'S LOVE

THE FATHER'S LOVE

*Amid a Frantic Search for His Son,
a Father finds His Faith.*

DAVE MOORE

TATE PUBLISHING & *Enterprises*

Published by Tate Publishing & Enterprises, LLC
127 E. Trade Center Terrace | Mustang, Oklahoma 73064 USA
1.888.361.9473 | www.tatepublishing.com

Tate Publishing is committed to excellence in the publishing industry. The company reflects the philosophy established by the founders, based on Psalm 68:11,
"The Lord gave the word and great was the company of those who published it."

Book design copyright © 2010 by Tate Publishing, LLC. All rights reserved.
Cover design by Lauran Levy
Interior design by Stefanie Rane

Published in the United States of America

ISBN: 978-1-61739-369-3
1. Religion, Christian Life, Family
2. Religion, Christian Life, Inspirational
10.12.03

DEDICATION

This book is dedicated to my wife Dorinda and Dr. Ricky Moore. Without your many hours of help, this book would not be a reality. Thank you.

ACKNOWLEDGMENTS

First my friend Larry Widener. Larry you are my best friend and closer then a brother. You have always been there for me. To my in-laws, Reverend G.J. (Chick) and Carla Chandler, I say thanks for never giving up on me. Your love and prayers were instrumental in bringing us all to God. Your true reward is in Heaven. Adam and Shane for putting up with me as your stepfather and now as one who won't shut up about how great God is. To my wife, Dorinda, I confess that there is no way that I could ever deserve how good you are to me. You are the love of my life. Your beauty and precious heart are such a gift from God. To my son, David, I would say that, from the first moment that you opened your eyes and looked at me, I was forever changed. I cannot explain how much you mean to me. I am more proud of you everyday as you live your life for God. The Stewart family,

Pastors Ron and Coleen, Justin and Jaime. In my early walk with God you were all so important in how you showed me the love of God. Your teachings have helped me to grow so much. My sister and brother-in-law, Dave and Toni Midura, John and Gloria Bishop, Randy and Lisa Root, All of you have been tireless workers for the Kingdom of God. You are all a shining light in the dark world we live in. Without your help, friendship, and great faith this book would not have been possible. Thank you. I love you all.

IN MEMORY OF

My Mom and Dad
Billy Gene and Wilma Jean Moore

My mom never let me down, was always there when I needed her and loved me no matter what. She was beautiful, funny, smart, witty, and was a defender of all that are oppressed. She never put herself first. I know she would have it no other way. My dad came from a poor farming family in Tennessee. He became a foreman at General Motors, built a beautiful house in northern Michigan, and for a time ran a small skateboard factory. I am proud of you, Dad, and thankful that we became close in the last years of your life. I will miss you both until we meet again in heaven.

Our Precious White German Shepherd
Tawnie

You were the best friend we ever had. You brought so much love to us (she was taken from us by cancer in June 2008). We will miss you forever.

TABLE OF CONTENTS

FOREWORD

This is a story told by a father about *the father's love*. It is very relevant to me for several "fatherly" reasons. I am a father too, and I am related to Dave, the father telling this story. Dave is my first cousin. Our fathers are brothers, so we both come from the same paternal grandfather, the late Reverend Ernest P. Moore. In addition to this, his father-in-law, Reverend G. J. Chandler, was my pastor throughout my teenage years, long before Dave came to be connected with him. At different points in our lives, then, this father-in-law has been a father-in-grace or a father-in-the-faith to both of us. Overarching all of this is the love of another father with whom Dave and I now share common lineage, our Father in heaven.

This is a story about how a father on earth lost connection with his son and at last got reconnected—reconnected to his son, yes, but also and only as he got reconnected to that fuller lineage that had for so long been reaching toward him, particularly through the faith, hope, and love of his father-in-law, his late grandfather, and ultimately from his Father in heaven.

Given the ultimate source, it is no wonder that the story Dave tells here bears a striking family resemblance to that story in Scripture we call *The Parable of the Prodigal Son.* The manifold truth of this parable now comes to us afresh and in a double way through Dave's story, for Dave is not only a father who finds his son but also a son who finds his Father.

I invite you to read these pages with the sincere hope and expectation that within them you too will find a fresh revelation of *the Father's love.*

RICKIE D. MOORE,
Professor of Old Testament
and Chair of the Department of Theology,
Lee University, Cleveland , TN

INTRODUCTION

My name is Dave Moore.

I was not raised in church. Though I had a limited amount of knowledge of the Bible, I always believed there was a God and very often would pray and ask for protection for my family. After college, I worked menial jobs. My main focus in life was to play softball and party. It was through these activities that I met the woman who would be the mother of my son, David. That relationship didn't last, but after two years, I took custody of my son, who was then one year old. After raising David alone for three years, I met my wife, Dorinda. She was in the process of a divorce and had two sons, Shane and Adam.

Dorinda had been raised in the church, saved and baptized at a young age. For several years, she had been away from God. She and I dated for two years and decided to get married. She told me that I would have to call her dad and ask his permission. Man, was that tough. She had asked both her parents to get on the phone because I wanted to talk to them. When I asked his permission to marry his daughter, there was a long silence. It seemed like an hour. Finally, Chick said that if I would promise to get his daughter back in church, he would give us his blessing. I agreed, but I guess I didn't really mean it. We were married on August 24, 1991.

For the next eleven years, the only time we went to church was when Chick came to Michigan for a revival. We always had an excuse. He would call us many Sundays to see if we had gone to church. When he called we would have an excuse already prepared. Then came the day when all of this would abruptly change. My son David graduated from High School in 2002. All of his teachers always said he was the smartest kid they had ever seen. Just like me, David loved to play sports. We did not raise David, Adam, and Shane in church, but I would occasionally see David in his room reading the Bible. David started college in the fall of 2002. I felt totally relaxed and confident that I had done a good job of raising my son. He was in college, had a job on campus, a girlfriend named Ashley, was driving a Mustang, and everything seemed perfect. It was—until the evening of December 6, 2002.

DAY ONE

Friday

The day began like most others. It was Friday. I got up that morning, made my lunch for work, and made it into work on time. It was a regular day at the warehouse. Work hard, get done, and get home. I got home from work about 3:30 p.m. My dog, Tawnie, a white German shepherd greeted me at the door. My son, David, was not home. That was not unusual. He had school that day, and many times he would stay after for his campus job or to play basketball.

I took Tawnie outside to play. It was an overcast, gloomy day. It was about to get a lot darker.

After playing with Tawnie, I came in to shower and relax. It was now about 5:30 p.m. My wife, Dorinda, would soon be home from work. Friday was pizza night. We would eat, probably watch a movie, and then retire for the night. Dorinda got home at 6:00 p.m. and Tawnie welcomed her. We had ordered the pizza, and it had just arrived.

As I began to eat, Dorinda walked into the room with a piece of paper in her hand. She said, "Haven't you been in David's room since you got home?" I said, "No." "David is gone," she said. Although the words my wife had just said did not make any sense to me, the look on her face did. Her face was as white as a ghost, and the look in her eyes had a sense of panic. As she reached towards me with a yellow sheet of paper, a horrible fear started to creep into my soul. David, my only child, a freshman at Eastern Michigan University, had left me a letter on his bed. Dorinda, after coming home from work, had walked into David's room to return a yearbook to his shelf, and that's when she discovered the letter. The letter said,

> *Dad, this is by far the most difficult decision I have ever had to make. I've come to this point by my own stupidity and laziness. I struggled this*

semester, by far the most I ever have throughout my schooling days. After realizing I couldn't salvage it, I've decided I need to leave. Although I love you with all my heart, I can't bear to see your reaction to my screw up. I would rather brave this tough world alone than feel like I've let you down or failed you. My frustration runs deep, and though it may seem like I am taking it out on you, I am not. It is just the fact that I don't know how else to handle my current situation. I figured if I kept it under wraps I could somehow turn it around. Please don't feel down or as if this is your fault. I've reached this point alone, and so I must deal with it alone too. Every bird has to leave the nest sometime; my time is now. I woke up every day hoping that I still had a chance to change it all. Thank you for all your support, and maybe one day this will all be behind me. Please don't hate me.

Love, David.

P.S. I'll keep in touch to let you know I'm okay.

P.S.S. The car is at the Greyhound station in Ann Arbor.

Since I began reading the letter tears had been pouring down my face. The fear, panic, and pain that I was feeling were overwhelming. My son, David, was gone. Immediately, I jumped up and told Dorinda to grab her purse. We were going to the bus station. I grabbed my keys and we took off. As we headed toward Ann Arbor, a trip of about twenty minutes, I was losing touch with reality. I was driving at a high rate of speed, running stop signs and red lights. I kept saying over and over, "What have I done? I pushed him too hard."

Dorinda, who always has had the cooler head, tried to calm me down. Even she was visibly shaking. I pulled my red Chevy Blazer to the front of the Greyhound bus station and jumped out—running to the door. I grabbed the door to open it, but it was locked. The sign on the door showed they had closed.

As I walked back to the Blazer, my mind was racing. What do I do now? I need to try to find David's car. As I pulled out to drive around and look for the car, I saw an Ann Arbor Police car driving towards me. I stopped my Blazer and got out to stop the police car. He looked puzzled at me approaching him, but as I told him what I was doing, he took action. He said for me to search the streets to the left, and he would search the streets to the right to try to locate David's car. Two streets over, Dorinda spotted David's car—a red 1994 Mustang parked on the street. Tears began to flow freely. He really did get on a bus. We had no idea about the destination.

We drove back to the bus station to meet with the policeman. He was on the radio with dispatch. We told him we had found David's Mustang. He informed us that dispatch was trying to contact Greyhound's main office, but without any luck. He asked if we had keys to David's car. We said we did. He thought we should take David's car home, and he would have his dispatch continue trying to contact Greyhound. He said that they would call us when they got in touch with them.

We drove back to get David's car. As I set down in David's driver's seat, I wondered how he must have felt when he got out of his car to get on that bus. Tears began again, falling off of my face onto my already wet shirt. As I started the car and began to drive home, the thought would not leave my head, *It's all your fault.* My mind was in chaos. How could I have pushed my son this way? Where could his bus be going? Is he suicidal? Will I ever see him again? I began to realize that I had a terrible headache and pain in my chest. My whole world had caved in. I thought about how much money David might be carrying. It couldn't be much. He would have his check from his campus job, but that wouldn't even be $100.00. Depending on how much his ticket cost, he would probably be broke when he got to his destination.

As we arrived home with the two vehicles, we realized home was not the same. Dorinda and I held each other and sobbed for a long time. Inside the house, Dorinda grabbed the Rolodex. We began to call David's friends in hopes of finding a clue to where he had gone. Ashley, David's girlfriend, was not home. We left a message and continued calling others. No one knew anything. After a short time, Ashley called back. She told me that she had felt like something had been wrong with David, but she had no idea he would do something like this. She then said that David, a week earlier, had mentioned something to her about the city of Dayton, Ohio. I thanked her and hung up.

My mind began racing. I knew I had to go to Dayton. I grabbed my wallet and keys and ran to the Blazer. I raced to the gas station to fill up. Even though I had just cashed my check, I headed to the bank for money from the teller machine. I had nearly stopped smoking cigarettes over the last six months. Now I began smoking one after the other. As I arrived back home, I saw Ashley's car at the house. She was inside, and she and Dorinda were crying. I grabbed what I needed to take to Dayton. Dorinda thought I needed someone to go with me, but there was no time for that. I gave them both a hug and started out the door. I was soon heading south on US-23 toward Dayton, Ohio.

It was hard to think clearly. What would I do when I got there? Where would I look? I didn't even know where to begin; I just knew that I had to go. How could this have happened? As far as I knew, everything was going well in David's life. I asked him every couple of days how things were going in school. He always said, "Good" or "Okay." I guess he didn't know how to tell me the truth. Fear gripped me. What if I never saw him again? If something happened to my son, I would take my own life. It would just be too much. Tears fell from my cheeks. The pain was unbearable. I had a constant pain in my chest for hours. I guess my heart was having trouble coping.

I looked down at the speedometer, and I was far over the speed limit. I couldn't slow down. I had to find my son. I had to get to Dayton. Just then, my cell phone rang. It was Dorinda. She told me that she and Ashley had been looking through David's room trying to find anything that might help. In David's trash can they found a piece of paper with an address on it. The address was to a homeless shelter in Dayton. "Oh God, that must be where he is going," I said. A feeling of exhilaration came over me. I now had hope. I had something to cling to. I sped the Blazer up, hitting ninety miles per hour. I thought, *I'm about an hour away. He must be there. Please, let him be there.* Dorinda and I continued to call each other every five minutes or so. But there still was no news.

DAY TWO

Saturday

Now after midnight, I came into the outskirts of Dayton. I saw flashing lights ahead. They were on the opposite side of the interstate. As I passed by, I saw that it was a police car stopped at an accident. I started looking for a road to turn back northbound. I could see one up ahead, and I turned onto it and headed back to the police car.

I had to talk with law enforcement and have them help me. I pulled up behind the police car, and the patrolman was standing outside next to his car. I approached him and began to fill him in on what had happened. He said he would be about five more minutes, and then he would lead me to the bus station. Five minutes seemed like an hour. Finally, he walked back to my car and said he was ready for me to follow him.

About fifteen minutes later, we pulled into the bus station. It was now 12:30 a.m. The station had closed at midnight. There was no one in sight anywhere. I informed the officer of the address that Dorinda and Ashley had found for the homeless shelter. He said he knew right where it was and to follow him there. The temperature was very cold. A bank sign read ten degrees. The streets were deserted. As we arrived at the homeless shelter, we made a U-turn and pulled up in front. I jumped out and ran up to the door. The policeman followed. There was a button next to a speaker, and I pushed it. A male voice asked if he could help me. I answered him that, yes, he could and I told him about my son and how we had found their address. He asked me David's age. "Eighteen years old," I responded. The voice informed me that David was an adult. The law would not allow him to tell me whether David was inside. I begged him to please tell me. He refused. He then told me that they make everyone leave the shelter at 7:00 a.m. If David were inside, he would have to come out then. I had over six hours to wait.

The policeman said there was another shelter about one mile away, and we should go there to look. I agreed, and we drove there and parked. As we knocked at the door, an older man opened it and asked us to come in. He said we could look through this shelter for David. I walked through the rows of cots and people sleeping on the floors. Some people's faces were showing, for others I had to lift blankets off of their faces to see them. I looked through the fifty or sixty people. None of them were my son.

As we left the building, the events of the last twenty hours began to catch up with me. I stumbled and fell down. The officer rushed to me and asked me if I was all right. I said yes and thanked him. I asked him to please take me back to the first shelter where I had to wait until 7:00 a.m. When we arrived back at the first shelter, the officer pulled up to the curb in front of the building. He told me that he had informed all the other patrol cars on duty about my situation. He had given them a description of my car and license plate number. If they saw me in town, they would know who I was and what I was doing. I thanked him for all his help.

I sat alone again, but I had hope that my son was inside the building not many feet away from where I was waiting. Looking at my phone, I noticed that my cell phone battery charge was very low. Calling home, I told Dorinda that we would have to call only when necessary until I could get my phone charged.

After about half an hour, I noticed someone walking about two hundred yards away. What if that was David? I started the Blazer and hurried down the street. As I got closer, I realized that this was not him. The bus station was on the left side of the road. I turned in and circled around the building. I saw nothing. Nobody was in sight. I headed back to the shelter. I was going the wrong way down a one-way street. I saw a police car parked on the road. I could see someone inside looking my way. The policeman waved at me. He must have known who I was and what I was doing. I pulled back in front of the shelter to begin my wait again. A little while later, I again noticed someone walking down the street far away. Could it be David this time? I headed down there. Again it was not David. I turned through the bus station and circled around. In the back of the bus station, I noticed a large cardboard box. Surely David was not inside there! I continued on past, not wanting to believe that for one second. I returned back to the shelter. This scenario would repeat itself several times as the night went on: see someone walking, hurry down there, turn around in the bus station, and come back to the shelter.

At 6:15 a.m. I again noticed someone walking. This time as I drove by I kept thinking about the cardboard box behind the bus station. What if David was in that box? I had to know. As I pulled around the back of the building, I turned my Blazer to shine my lights on the box. It was big enough to hold someone. I climbed out of the Blazer and slowly walked toward it. There was a lid on top. I reached out and slowly lifted the lid. It was very dark inside. As my eyes focused, I could begin to see that someone was in there. "David," I said. There was movement. I began to make out a face. It was not David. An older, gray-haired man looked up at me. He seemed to have several layers of clothes on in the ten-degree weather. He looked at me with very sad and tired eyes and said, "No, I am not David." I told him I was sorry, but he did not reply. I gently let down the lid to his box and returned to my Blazer. The thought of my son being in this situation shook me to my core. As I drove back to the shelter, I was again sobbing uncontrollably.

It was almost 7:00 a.m. I waited outside the shelter with my eyes fixed on the doorway. As 7:00 a.m. finally came, the door remained closed. Five minutes passed, then ten. Finally at 7:15, the front door opened. Slowly one by one, people began to walk out and head down the street—young people, old people, men, women, black, and white, all aspects of life, but no David. I got out and began to ask the homeless people if they remembered seeing my son. They all said no. They wanted to help me. A middle-aged man went back in the shelter to see if everyone had left. He came back with the shelter director. He informed me that there was no one left inside. I was devastated. A feeling of helplessness came over me. What could I do now?

As I started to walk back to my Blazer, I sank down and sat on the curb. A young girl in her twenties and the man that had helped me came and sat beside me. The homeless were comforting me. They told me I must keep my hopes up. They said there was a day shelter that they were going to. If my son were in Dayton outside in this weather, he would probably make his way there. I tried to thank them by giving them money, but they refused it. They told me to follow them as they made their way to the day shelter. I really can't believe that they refused my offer to give them money. They really did just want to help me. Amazing.

As I followed them to the day shelter, I decided to call Dorinda and tell her what I had found out. She informed me that she and Ashley had been up all night trying to figure out what was missing from David's room and what he would be wearing. They believed David was most likely wearing jeans, a t-shirt, his red and white varsity jacket, and a black baseball cap. He was also carrying his backpack and two duffle bags. I had to hang up because my phone was nearly dead.

When we arrived at the day shelter, I noticed people coming from all directions to the building. As I walked into the building, I noticed that it was already getting crowded. There was a desk straight ahead with a young man seated behind it.

I waited in line to talk to him. When I finally got to the desk, I told him why I was there. He told me I was welcome to stay and look for David as long as I wanted. I walked around examining all of the faces. Most of the people seemed very friendly in spite of their circumstances. There were two rooms. I looked at everyone in both rooms, but David was not there.

I saw an outlet to plug in my phone, and there was an open seat nearby. I called Dorinda again and told her where I was and what I was doing. As I was hanging up the phone with Dorinda, the homeless man who had been helping me walked up. He had a sandwich and a cup of coffee for me. Again, he was helping *me*. But I was unable to eat it. Though one might think that by now I should have run out of tears, this was not the case. He told me not to give up. I thanked him and told him I would not give up.

I started thinking about what to do next. The bus station sign had shown that they would reopen at 9:00 a.m. At 8:30 there was still no sign of David. I unplugged my phone and stuck the charger in my pocket. I had learned that the homeless man's name was Leon. I told Leon of my plan. I would head back to the bus station and try to find out anything I could about David's bus ticket. I thanked him for all his help and concern. I pulled my money out of my pocket. I told Leon I wanted to give him some. He flat out refused. I insisted. He would not take one dollar. I went back to the desk and asked the young man if he would keep a look out for my son. He took a description of David and my phone number and wrote it on an index card. He then pinned it on a bulletin board with all the others. It did not give me any peace.

Back in my Blazer, I headed back to the Greyhound station. As I was passing by a restaurant, I noticed a police car in the parking lot. I wondered if this was the day shift and if they knew about my situation. I turned into the parking lot. As I entered the building, I scanned the area for the officers. They were on the far side of the room seated at a table. I first asked them to forgive me for interrupting them, and then I started to fill them in on the details. One of the officers took out a notepad and made notes. They told me they were unaware of this and thanked me for informing them. They said they would help any way they could. As I turned around and walked toward the door, suddenly a hand grabbed hold of my left arm stopping me. Startled, I looked over at the man who had grabbed my arm. He was crying. He told me that he was sorry, but that he couldn't help but overhear my conversation with the police officers. He then asked me if he could pray for me. I said, "Please do." He took both of my hands in his and began to pray out loud. Right in the middle of that packed restaurant while we both openly wept, he prayed a wonderful prayer for me and my son. When he finished, he hugged me and said he would continue to pray for us. As I wiped my face dry again, I thanked him and headed out the door.

Pulling up to the bus station, I noticed that people were already going inside. I looked at my watch and it was 9:10 a.m. There was a line at the counter. I was fifth in line. Finally, I reached the counter. A young, friendly-looking man was working the counter. I started telling him my story. He stopped me and told me to come around the counter. He called to another worker and had an older man start helping those who were still in line.

My phone rang. It was Dorinda. She wanted to know if anything new had happened. As we talked, I realized that my phone was running out of battery again. We had been calling each other nearly every twenty minutes. Calvin, the Greyhound worker, overheard that my cell phone battery was dying. He had me plug it in behind the counter. I hung up with Dorinda, and Calvin motioned for me to follow him. He walked to a computer and began to type. He asked for David's full name and the location where he boarded the bus. After a couple of moments, he turned to look at me with a not-so-hopeful look. David's ticket that was purchased in Ann Arbor, Michigan was to have arrived in Atlanta, Georgia thirty minutes ago.

Right then, a customer upset about waiting, yelled out at Calvin to hurry up and help him. Calvin snapped back and told him to shut up, that he was helping me. Calvin jumped into action. He immediately looked up the phone number of the Atlanta Greyhound station where David's bus had just arrived. He dialed the number. No answer. He hung up and dialed again. No answer. Now, getting frustrated, he hung up and dialed again. Someone answered. Calvin told the person on the other end that this was an emergency. He told them who he was and to immediately page David Moore over their public address system. We waited. A few minutes went by. Finally the person in the Atlanta station came back to the phone. No David Moore had come forward. He asked them to page the name again. We waited again. Nothing. No one came forward. Calvin gave them the bus number and asked if it had arrived on time. It had. If David had arrived there, he was already gone. Calvin thanked them and hung up.

The feeling of hope that had started to rise completely left me. I leaned my back against the wall. The hopelessness and the full weight of no sleep, no food, no water, hit me all at once. My legs began to shake. I slid down the wall and sat before I fell. Calvin came and sat beside me. He put his arm around my shoulder. "What do I do? I have no strength. I am so weak. My whole world has caved in on me. Atlanta feels like it is on the other side of the world."

I asked Calvin to use their phone to call Dorinda. When she answered, I told her the details of what had happened. She couldn't believe it. I told her I didn't know what to do. She didn't know either. I didn't know how I could make it to Atlanta. We finally decided that I must come back home to Michigan to get some rest. I thanked

Calvin and got my phone to head home. I got Calvin's phone number and told him that I would let him know what happened.

Outside, I climbed into my Blazer and made my way back to I-75 north toward Michigan. This just did not feel good or right. After driving one mile, I got off at the next exit. I turned back onto I-75 south heading to Atlanta. I called Dorinda and told her I had changed my mind. David was in Atlanta, and I couldn't come back to Michigan without trying to find him. She didn't think that I could make it. I agreed with her, but I told her I had to try. She told me that she and Ashley would get on the computer and get me directions and anything else they could do. I hung up to try to save the little bit of charge left in my phone.

As I began to think about the task that I had before me, I became more and more depressed. How would I ever make the drive? When I got there, if I got there, how would I find David? What had I done? This was all my fault. How could I run my son away, maybe forever? What if I never saw him again? What if he kills himself? It's all my fault. I began to have thoughts of taking my own life. The pain in my head, in my heart, in my very soul, had become nearly unbearable. I began to look at the bridges as I passed them. I thought it would be easy. I could just speed up and drive into the next one. I deserved it. I thought, *Look what I've done to my own son.* I stepped on the gas. I made up my mind. It was the only way out. I could see the next bridge approaching.

Suddenly, a thought came to my mind. What if David was alive? What would it do to David if I killed myself? He would never recover; never forgive himself. I took my foot off of the gas and began to slow down. My eyes were so full of tears I could hardly see. I pulled over on the side of the road. After a few minutes, I got back on the highway and headed to Atlanta.

Seeing a sign ahead for Lexington, Kentucky, I remembered my good friend, Larry Widener, lived there. I called Dorinda and told her to call Larry's house and tell him that I needed his help. A few minutes later, Larry called my cell phone. Larry told me that he is never home on Saturday morning, but on that day he was sitting right next to the phone when Dorinda called. He told me to come and get him; he was going with me to Atlanta. As he began to give me directions to his home, I felt a new surge of hope. The roller coaster ride of emotions I had been on had taken a direction up again. Just in time to save my life.

As I pulled up in to Larry's driveway, he was coming out the door. He was literally a sight for sore eyes. Larry was my best friend in the whole world. Even though we now lived hundreds of miles apart, we were still closer than brothers. In our younger days, we were real hell raisers, but we could always depend on each other in any situation. I knew that I could still trust Larry with my life.

As we met in the yard, Larry gave me a big hug. He said he was almost ready to leave. I told him that I wanted to stop at a RadioShack and get a car charger for my phone. When he was ready, we set out for RadioShack. I also needed to fill up with gas and cigarettes. I was still chain-smoking one right after the other. Larry took over the driving, and we pointed the Blazer south on I-75 to Atlanta.

I called Dorinda and told her we were on our way. I asked her if there was any news on her end. She said that she and Ashley had been on the Internet using David's screen name. They had been making contact with as many of David's friends as possible. When they told them who they were, and that David was missing, none of them believed it. They all thought it was some kind of joke or hoax. No one thought David would ever do such a thing. Neither did we. I told her to keep trying and call me with any news at all. She said that she would and would give me the directions to the Greyhound station in Atlanta when we got closer to it.

We were probably six hours away. I tried to close my eyes and rest. I had been awake now for over thirty hours. I still had not eaten anything and had hardly drunk anything. I couldn't sleep; my mind was still racing. What would we do when we got there? What if he had started to hitchhike to Florida where it was warmer? Anything was possible. I asked Larry what he thought we should do when we got there. He said we should go to the bus station and get as much information as possible. Then we could search every street in town until we found David. Larry's confidence that we would find him was much needed. I didn't think it could overcome my negative attitude, but at least it might slow it down. Just having him with me was a huge help.

Larry began to talk about old times when we played softball, partied, got in fights, and experienced the so-called good old days. This temporary change of subject was just what I needed. We began to reminisce about the past, and we actually began to have a few laughs. Then reality kicked back in, and I began to cry all over again. I felt the speed of the Blazer pick up. I thought Larry was beginning to feel some of the desperation I had been feeling for the last thirty hours or so.

The road was endless. Mile after mile seemed to go so slow. I stared down at the highway, not even noticing any of the landscape on the side of the road. I began to think of David. What was he thinking as the bus traveled down this very road? Was he depressed? Angry? Scared? Did he want to turn around and come home? Did he never want to come home? Did he know how much I loved him? Did he care? I had to find him. My life depended on it. Fear again took over. I angrily swung my fist into the dashboard. Larry didn't say a word, but I could feel him looking at me. I looked over at him without saying anything.

Larry started pulling the Blazer off at the next exit. I asked him what he was doing. He said he needed something to eat, and so did I. I told him I couldn't eat; my stomach was in knots. He asked me to please try. He pulled into a fast food drive-through and ordered for both of us. After paying, he got right back on the road, heading for Atlanta. He again asked me to try to eat something. I handed him a hamburger and took one myself. As I tried to eat, my stomach didn't seem to accept the food. I ate about half of the hamburger, and that was all I could take.

My phone rang. It was Dorinda. We again asked each other if there was any news. She told me that she had contacted her parents in Alabama. Her father, Rev. G. J. Chandler, is a national evangelist for the Church of God. She asked them to pray and ask God to help us. They said they would contact others and all began a prayer chain. We would find out later that this prayer chain would end up stretching nationwide. I told her that this was good because we could use all the help we could get. We promised to keep each other informed and hung up.

After a couple of hours, we were finally getting close to Atlanta. I had to call Dorinda back and get directions to the bus station that David's bus ticket indicated. It was dark outside now. I thought about him being on these streets alone.

Getting closer to the bus station, we noticed that there were more and more people on the streets. It was much warmer here than it was in Dayton. Driving slowly, we scanned the streets and faces looking for my son. Most of these people were young, black males. It was somewhat easy to pick out the occasional white face. Every time we saw one, we slowed down to take a look. Turning onto the street where the bus station was we could see people everywhere. There were fifty to a hundred people within a block of the station. They all looked to be street people. The looks on their faces were not the same as the homeless people in Dayton. These people had angry, evil looks as they stared at us driving slowly down the street.

There was a parking lot next to the bus station. Larry swung the Blazer into the lot and parked. Eyes from every direction were staring at us. As we exited the Blazer, I was unafraid. I had to find my son. Nothing was going to stop me. Larry and I started walking toward the bus station and about ten young men headed toward us from different directions. When the first one got close to us, he looked at me and asked if I had any money. I reached in my pocket and pulled out a wad big enough to choke a horse. All the others gathered around me. I told them that I was looking for my son. I gave them all money—ones, fives, tens. I told them that if they found my son I would give them all of the rest of the money I had on me. Their eyes were as big as pancakes as they watched us walk into the bus station. Larry looked at me and told me how stupid that was. I told him that they had no clue what a mistake that would be messing with me right now. I seriously felt like a caged lion.

Right then, a voice behind me said loudly, "Hey." I turned around and saw one of the men to whom I had given money standing there. He said that he knew where my son was. He said if I would follow him across the street to the alley, he would tell me where David was. I told him to tell me right there. He said no. I pulled the wad of money out of my pocket. I told him that if he wanted it, to tell me right now. Just then I saw a police car pull up out front. I said to Larry that maybe the police could help. The homeless man walked away quickly.

Larry and I met the two policemen walking into the bus station. When I started to talk to them, they told me to wait. They had other business first. They approached the ticket counter and began talking to a middle-aged lady working there. She seemed to be very angry. Everyone in this town seemed to be angry. When the policemen finished talking at the ticket counter, they walked over to us. I started telling them what had happened. He asked if I would mind walking back to their car and talking to them there. When we got to his car, he opened the back door and Larry and I got in. I could see people everywhere looking at the car. I began to tell them what we were doing as one of the officers took notes. When I finished, the officer taking the notes got on the radio and started talking to his dispatch. When he was done, he told me that they had sent a detective down to talk to me. He said we should wait in the station until the detective arrived. He warned us that these street people were extremely dangerous, and we should not trust them or turn our backs on them for one second.

We returned inside and took a seat in the back. After waiting about five minutes, I walked to the counter to talk to the lady working there. I asked her if she had been working there this morning when the Dayton office had them page the name David Moore. She very rudely said she was not working then. I told her that my son had run away from Michigan and was most likely here on these streets—broke and alone. She stared at me without saying a word and then broke down and started crying. She said that she was so sorry that she had been rude to me, but that she had had such a bad day. I told her that I had had a bad day too. She nodded her head that she understood. She told me that she had a printout of shelters where I could look for David. I thanked her as she gave me several sheets of paper with the names of shelters in the area. I took them and returned to where Larry was sitting.

Soon a young man in a suit came in and began asking for me. I jumped up and walked to him, introducing myself. It was the detective we were waiting for , Tom O'Neil. I again told the story of what had happened. The detective told me that even though he was taking a report, I had to go back to Michigan to file an actual missing persons report. He said that there were thousands of people on these streets, and it would be nearly impossible to find him. He also gave me a list of shelters and wished me luck. Before he left, he gave me his card and told me to call him when I found out anything.

Armed with our list of shelters, we started back to the Blazer to begin our search. As we reached the parking lot, a new group of people quickly descended on us. This time there were about fifteen people. They seemed to be led by two white males in their late twenties. I again produced the wad of cash and began giving everyone in the group some. I told them that if they found my son, I would give them the rest. One of the two leaders spoke up and asked me what David looked like. I told him David was about 6'1", around 170 pounds, light brown medium length hair, probably carrying at least two duffle bags. He told me that he saw him at the bus station today. I asked him where he thought he could have gone. He didn't know. He said I should give him the money. I said that he hadn't helped find him. He said that he still deserved the money. Shouting, I said that if he found David I would give him all my money. Realizing my desperation, the group backed off.

Larry and I got in the Blazer. As we started driving up the street, there was a bridge ahead of us and I could see people up under the bridge. I told Larry to pull over. Jumping out, I ran up the hill to look under the bridge. There were ten or so people under the bridge in the darkness. I could barely make them out. I yelled out "Is David Moore up here?" No one answered. Saying it again, I bent down and walked underneath the bridge. I started telling them I was looking for my son and that I would give them money if they helped me find him. I reached into my pocket pulling out the money and giving each of them some. I went back down to Larry to continue our search.

Slowly Larry and I drove down the streets. There were people walking, standing, and sitting everywhere. We saw an outdoor mall that sat back off the road about a hundred feet. There were many young adults congregating in the open-air walkways between the stores. I told Larry to let me out and find somewhere to park. As I got out, I saw a young white male about David's height walking about fifty feet away. He was carrying a duffle bag. I hurried to catch up to him. As I got closer, I realized it was not David. I sat down on a cement wall looking at the faces as they walked by. Larry came walking up and sat next to me. We watched the people walking back and forth. While watching for David, we began talking about what our next step would be. Larry brought up the possibility of David having gotten off the bus at a stop between Ann Arbor and Atlanta. He also said he could have arrived in Atlanta and immediately started hitchhiking to Florida. I knew that all this was possible. It felt like we were looking for a needle in a haystack. I got up and started walking, and Larry followed. We walked down the street looking in every direction. Nothing. We went back to the Blazer to drive the streets again.

I began to look at the list of shelters. Some were nearby. We decided to look at the ones closest to the bus station. As we traveled to the first shelter, we stopped at two bridges along the way. I walked up the hill, scanned the faces, and asked the homeless about seeing my son. Same results. No one knew anything. When we arrived at the first shelter, we were invited inside to look. There were about twenty-five people inside of all ages and races, but no David. Returning outside, I noticed a large box between two dumpsters. I opened the box and an older man looked up at me. I apologized for disturbing him. Without saying a word, he reached up and pulled the box lid back down. Larry and I looked at each other and just shook our heads in disbelief. This city was the saddest place I had ever been in my life. We returned to the Blazer and looked for the next shelter. This scenario continued for hours—looking in shelters, under bridges, and inside more boxes. There was still no clue as to where David was. I had given away money, cigarettes, promises, anything I knew to give—tears, hugs, sweat, everything that I had. Nothing. Not a clue, not a lead, and not a hope.

DAY THREE

Sunday

I t was now early in the morning on Sunday. Larry and I came to the last shelter we would search in Atlanta. A well-spoken, well-dressed man around thirty years old answered the shelter's front door. After telling him about David, he began to cry. He said he had only about six people inside and that they were all black men. He said that he felt so sorry for me and that he would pray that God would help me to find my son. He was an attorney, and he gave me his card and asked if I would call him whenever I heard anything about David. I assured him that I would let him know, and I turned and went back to the Blazer. Back inside the truck, Larry and I sat there in silence. Larry, a few years older than I, was several hours past his bedtime. I had been up now for more than forty-five hours with no sleep.

We were feeling like we had come to a dead end. We were exhausted, discouraged, and not even sure whether David was in Atlanta. I asked Larry to drive around some more and make our way back to the bus station. Even though it was now 2:00 a.m., there were still people walking all over the city. We slowed to look at faces, sometimes stopping to look. Still nothing. We made two passes around the block where the bus station was.

The Atlanta police detective had said that I should file a missing police report back in Michigan. We finally decided to end our search here in Atlanta. It was time to take Larry home, and go back to Michigan. It was the hardest choice I had ever made in my life. Back on the highway, headed north away from Atlanta, I kept second guessing myself. I felt like I was abandoning my son. Should we turn back and look some more? Maybe we should get a room and start fresh in the morning. I couldn't decide. Larry couldn't either.

We kept driving. Hours passed. Crying came and went. I continued to call home every half hour or so. No news. Nothing. Finally, early in the morning, we arrived back in Lexington at Larry's house. I had to try to sleep.

Larry's wife, Robin, met us at the door. She asked us what had happened. Larry told her some of what we had done, but we couldn't find David. Robin turned to me with tears in her eyes and hugged me. She told me how sorry she was. She led me downstairs to a bedroom where I could sleep. She told me I must eat and went back upstairs to make me some food. When she returned with some food, I did my best to try to eat, but I was still not able. Finally, I just lay down on the bed. Robin placed a cold washcloth on my head and turned out the light. As she left, I felt as alone and broken as anyone could imagine.

Sleep came in ten or fifteen minute periods, never lasting longer. After about three hours of this, I got up, went upstairs, and told Larry and Robin that I must drive home. They both let me know that anything they could do, they would do. I hugged them and left to drive back to Michigan. I didn't know how, but I seemed to be wide-awake.

A new determination had risen up in me. I needed to get the police in Michigan involved. I needed to get as many people to help me as I could.

I began to think of what my next moves would be. I would contact the Washtenaw County Sheriff's Department first. I could file the missing person report with them. I would contact John Walsh, famous for helping to find missing children. I would go to Eastern Michigan University and talk to David's teachers and fellow students. I could post his picture all over campus. I had to get back home and get started.

The drive home again seemed to be endless. My mind was a battleground of extremes. Ideas of what to do next to help find David seemed constantly to flood my thinking. Yet the negative side, thinking the worst of what might have happened to my son, was always occupying my mind.

Friends and family had been in constant contact with Dorinda, offering prayers and any help that they could. David's friends had started to call, realizing that he really had disappeared and that this wasn't a joke. Everyone was at a loss to understand why this had happened.

I finally arrived home and pulled into the driveway. Dorinda stepped into view in the front door along with Tawnie, my precious white German Shepherd. It was good to see them, yet it was not a joyful return. I had come home the same way that I left—alone. Tawnie came running down the porch steps to see me. Dorinda had come down also, and Ashley had appeared in the front door. After our brief reunion, we went back into the house. The girls looked tired. They had been awake about as much as I had. We all agreed that it was time to call the police and make a missing person report on David. Dorinda found the Washtenaw County Sheriff's Department phone number. When I called, the female voice on the other end asked if this was an emergency. I told them yes, my son was missing. She took my name and address and said she would send someone over as soon as possible.

The girls filled me in on some of the conversations they had had with our family and David's friends during the previous two days. Dorinda's sons, Adam and Shane, had both been to the house Saturday and this morning to offer their help. My mother, Jean, also had been in contact with Dorinda trying to offer her help in anyway. She had been a strong emotional support. Most had been concerned and offered help but had little idea on how to help.

I picked up the phone and called Larry. I wanted to tell him that I had made it home safely. Larry answered and told me that he had been in contact with his brother, Bruce. Bruce worked for the federal government and wanted to help. Larry gave me Bruce's phone number and asked me to call him. Bruce's wife answered the phone and called for Bruce. She told me how sorry she was and that she would be praying for us. I thanked her and waited. Bruce came to the phone and asked me to tell him what had happened. I again told the story of how David had disappeared. He told me that if I could give him a description of David, along with a picture, he would have it faxed to every police agency from Michigan to Florida. Giving me his fax number, he told me to fax it Monday morning. I told him that I would get a flyer together describing David and fax it to him the next day. I also told him how thankful I was for all his help.

I hung up and the girls and I begin writing down information describing David. White male, eighteen years old, 6'1" tall, slim build, 175 pounds, brown medium length hair, blue eyes, wearing blue jeans, t-shirt, black baseball hat, with red letters WR on front, carrying two or three bags. Dorinda got one of David's graduation pictures.

I got an idea to call the police department in Florida. David could be hitchhiking that way. I called information and got the number for the Florida State Patrol. A man answered, and I began to give him information about David. He told me that it was illegal to hitchhike in Florida and that they would pick him up and hold him for vagrancy if they found him with no money. He assured me that they would call me if they found him. Thanking him, I hung up and lay down on the sofa. It felt like we were making some progress, yet I was still exhausted, worried, weak, and feeling lost. I didn't know how I could keep going on.

Tawnie ran to the front window barking. The sheriff's officer had arrived. We hustled Tawnie into the bedroom and let the officer in. The young female officer, Sandy Rowley, was very friendly. She took all of our information and was very positive. She tried to comfort us. She assured us that she would contact the Atlanta Police Detective and coordinate the investigation with him. We informed her about the help of our friend, Bruce, and his faxing David's information to all of the police departments. Deputy Rowley told us that she would be contacting the State Police computer-investigating unit. They would soon come to our house and investigate our computer files for any information that might help them find David. They thought it was possible that someone might have talked to David over the Internet and enticed him to go to Atlanta. We had never thought of this. The officer got up to leave, and we thanked her and saw her to the door.

As we all returned and sat down, we realized how lost we still were. We all looked at each other in disbelief. Though we seemed to have come a long way, we really were no closer than when we started. Dorinda began to cry. I put my arm around her, and Ashley came over to the couch and sat with us. We all sat quietly together without saying a word.

As the afternoon slowly moved toward evening, I decided to look over the list of shelters that I had brought back from Atlanta. One-by-one, I started calling the shelters on the list. As I called each shelter, I began by telling them the story of David's disappearance, and I ended by giving them a description of David. I asked them if they had a fax number where I could send a flyer to them. Most were very helpful and seemed anxious to help.

After working on the lists for a couple of hours, I began to get really tired. Ashley had gone home to check in with her family. While sitting on the couch, Dorinda and I both fell asleep. We slept for many hours, waking up in the middle of the night. Ashley had returned and was asleep in the chair. Dorinda went to the computer to check for any messages for or from David. A few of David's friends had left messages but nothing of any importance. Waking up, Ashley told us that she had talked to friends of hers and David's. None of them knew anything that could help us find him. We decided to go to bed and wake up fresh in the morning and begin our search again. Ashley went to David's room to sleep in his bed. Though sleep was dearly needed, it was not welcomed, for even in sleep I was tormented.

DAY FOUR

Monday

I woke up and looked at the clock; it was 7:00 a.m. Monday morning. It had been about sixty hours, two and a half days, since David left. It felt like much longer. I decided that I would start my day by going to Eastern Michigan University and talking to the officials there. Looking at Tawnie, I realized that I had really been neglecting her. I hadn't taken her for a walk and had hardly even petted her. She had been right by my feet everywhere I had gone and yet until then I had hardly noticed her. As I took her outside, she was really excited. She wandered across my neighbor's yard along her usual trail. She was glad to get back into her normal routine. How I would love to be back into mine.

Back inside, I hurriedly showered and got dressed. I was hoping that I might get some answers at David's college. Dorinda woke up and asked what my plans were. I told her that I was going to Eastern's campus to do anything I could. She said that she would go to her work and make up the posters to place around Eastern's campus. She was going to fax a poster to Bruce and all of the shelters we had fax numbers for.

As I drove to the Eastern Michigan campus, I was not sure where to begin. Pulling onto campus, I saw a sign for the police headquarters. I thought that was a good place to start. After parking the car, I went inside the police department and saw there were several officers there. The officer at the counter asked if he could help me. I told him that I hoped he could, and I began to tell the story once again. All the officers stopped talking and began to listen intently as I recounted what had happened up to then.

When I finished telling the story, I asked the officer if it would be possible to talk to David's teachers. He picked up the phone and talked to someone in the counseling department. They told him to send me over to talk to them. After giving me directions, the officer told me they would do everything they could to help.

My cell phone rang. It was Dorinda. She had the copies of David's poster. I told her to meet me at Eastern and bring thumbtacks and tape so we could hang the posters all over campus.

Waiting in the car, I closed my eyes and began to think back on what had transpired up to that point. I had been to Dayton, Ohio, and waited outside the homeless shelter all night. I had gone to Lexington, Kentucky and picked up Larry on my way to Atlanta, Georgia. After driving to Atlanta, we had spent all night and early morning walking the streets, handing out money, and searching shelters. We had then driven back to Lexington, Kentucky, and I drove back to Michigan. I had talked to the Ann Arbor Police, the Dayton Police, the Atlanta Police and Detectives, the Florida Highway Patrol, the Washtenaw County Sheriffs Department, and numerous shelters. I had also emailed John Walsh. Larry's brother Bruce was now faxing the poster to every police department from Michigan to Florida. I had talked to the Eastern Michigan University Police Department and soon would be talking to the Michigan State Police about searching my computer.

Dorinda pulled up next to me. She had a stack of posters and a bag of pins and tape. I filled her in on my meeting with the campus police. We parted ways; I went to talk to David's teachers; Dorinda was going home where she and Ashley could go back online and try to contact people who might know David.

I arrived in the counseling department and was greeted there by a young woman. As I told her why I was there, she asked me to wait while she went to get the department head. Mrs. Smith, the chair of the department, returned and informed me that the campus police had somewhat filled her in on what had happened. She asked me to come into her office and sit down. Inside her office, I asked her if it were possible to talk with David's teachers and address his classes. She said that she would call and encourage all the teachers to allow me to do that. As she began to call all the teachers, tears began to roll down her cheeks. She hung up the phone, and we both began to cry. She grabbed a box of tissue and came to sit in the chair beside me. After a few minutes, we recovered and she returned to the phone. One after another, all of David's teachers agreed to allow me to address the classes. I could visit two today and two tomorrow.

Mrs. Smith asked me to fill her in on everything that I knew about what had happened. She wanted to know if there had been any problems at home or anywhere else. I told her that there was nothing that I knew of. After giving her as much information as I could, I thanked her for all her help and for her compassion. She gave me permission to put up David's poster anywhere on campus. As I came out of her office, there were others standing around talking. They said they were so sorry and prayed everything would turn out okay. I thanked them and went back to my car. I had about an hour before addressing David's first class. I wanted to go home and get the letter David left us, so I could read it to the students. As I drove home, I felt like I was doing all of the right things.

Right before I pulled into the driveway at my house, a thought came to my mind. My friend at work, Jim Lee, had talked to me about visiting a psychic to try to talk to his brother who had passed away. He had told me that he thought that he had made contact with his brother on more than one occasion. I was always very skeptical about it, yet I was willing to try anything to find David.

When I got inside the house, I started looking for Jim's phone number. Finding it, I immediately called him. Jim answered, and I asked him to give me the psychic's phone number. It took only a minute, and he was giving me the number. When I called, a girl answered and I asked her if I could make an appointment. She wanted to know what I wanted exactly. I told her that my son was missing. She said the earliest appointment she had was the next day, Tuesday, at 4:30 pm. I made the appointment and hung up. In a hurry now, I grabbed the letter David wrote us and drove back to Eastern Michigan campus to talk to David's first class.

As I started out the back door, I heard Dorinda call my name. She told me that she had just remembered that Shawn Rafferty, an attorney that once worked at her office, had moved to Atlanta, Georgia. She said she would call him and see about faxing him a poster and asking him if he knew of any way that he might be able to help.

I hurriedly drove back to Eastern to try to talk to David's teacher before the class started. Jogging in to the building, I made it to the class a few minutes before it started. The teacher asked me if I had heard any news about David yet. I told her that I hadn't. Slowly the students were beginning to trickle into the lecture hall. As we waited for all the students to arrive, I continued to give the teacher more details of what had happened. I was becoming more emotional and nervous as the lecture hall filled up. Finally, the teacher walked to the front and told the class who I was and that I would like to talk to them. I then told them about how David had left home, and how I had tried to find him. Following this, I read his letter. I continually had to fight back the tears as I told the story. Nearly everyone in the class, it seemed, was wiping tears from their faces. When I finished, I asked if anyone knew anything that could help me find David. No one knew anything. As I turned around to thank the teacher for letting me address the class, I realized that she had been crying too. She walked up to me and gave me a hug and told me she would be praying for David's safe return. I thanked her and the class and then left.

Since I had some time before David's next class, I walked to different buildings, posting David's flyer everywhere I could. I put it up on doors, bulletin boards, and on car windshields. After a while, I saw that it was getting close to the next class, so I hurried to make it there in time. The talk with the next class was nearly identical to the first one. Nobody knew anything. Again many of the students started crying. The teacher asked me to please let him know how it all turned out. I assured him that I would. Thanking him, I left for home. On my way, I stopped at a few more buildings and put up more flyers.

When I arrived home, I saw Tawnie looking out the front door. I let her out and bent down to hug her. She was happy to see me and licked me all over the face. I sat out on the front yard with her, and we wrestled around and played. It was a temporary relief from my nightmare. Dorinda came out and then so did Ashley. We all took a brief break from what we had been dealing with. Tawnie loved the attention. Dorinda told me that she had talked to Shawn and his wife Vickie in Atlanta. He gave her his fax number and said when she faxed David's poster, they would put it up around town. Vickie also gave us information about putting an advertisement in a weekly Atlanta newspaper that David might see.

We went inside, and while Dorinda made us something to eat, I filled them in on my talks with the teachers and students. Through the posters being seen and the students spreading the word, I thought that if there was anyone who knew anything, we would eventually hear from them.

After trying to eat, I got my list of shelters and began to call and re-call people on the list. We had been getting more and more calls from family and friends wanting to help. My sister, Cindy, called from Houston, Texas. She is a nurse there. She had begun a process of checking with hospitals in Atlanta and the surrounding areas looking for David.

After hanging up with Cindy, I went out on the front porch to smoke a cigarette. I had still been smoking nearly two packs a day. I decided to go next door and talk to my neighbors. Maybe they had seen something. Mrs. Abukaff was home, along with her son Raed. I told them what had happened, and she began to cry. She told me how sorry she was and how bad she felt for us. I could tell that she really meant it. Raed told me that he would do anything he could to help me, anything at all. I knew that they would. I left them, promising to let them know if I found out anything or if I needed anything.

I walked next door to my other neighbors, the Osborne's, though I didn't know Dorinda had already talked to them. Kim Osborne said her church had been praying already. She offered to help in any way that we needed. I thanked her and went back home.

While I was gone, the Washtenaw County Sheriffs Department had called. They had been in contact with the Atlanta Police Department. They were coordinating the investigation, and they felt confident that they would find David. I have always been a pessimistic person, and I had never been less confident in my life. I literally felt that there was not one drop of positive blood in my body right then.

The phone rang, and it was Larry calling from Lexington. I told him that there was no news. He told me that he would be praying for us. I had never heard Larry say anything about God or praying before. It struck me as kind of funny. I looked in front of me, and there was a Bible sitting there. I thought to myself, how I wish that I knew God and that I could ask him to help me.

The doorbell rang. I jumped up from the table and ran to the door. It was my neighbor, Raed, and his uncle. They told me that if I went back to Atlanta that they were going to go back with me—no ifs, ands, or buts. I thanked them and told them that I would like that very much. They both gave me a hug and walked back next door. People were really trying to help.

My mom had been by several times, and she had really tried to be positive. She had always been a rock. Our house phone and cell phones had been ringing nearly non-stop. It was hard to keep all of the phones charged. Dorinda's sister, Darla, and her husband, Jerry Shepherd, pastor of the Church of God in Durand, Michigan had asked their church to pray. Also, Dorinda's brother, Ed Chandler, pastor of the Church of God in Lapeer, Michigan, and his wife were praying too.

It had been about seventy-two hours at that point, and as far as I knew we were no closer than we were at the beginning. Time seemed to have no meaning or place in our lives. We had not worked, and we had slept very little. Both of our employers had said to take as much time as we needed. Every time we heard the phone or doorbell ring, we were hoping that it was David. Right then, nothing else mattered. It was getting dark outside again. I wondered if David was outside in the dark and cold. The thought was too terrible to think about. Was he cold? Hungry? Lost? I didn't know how much more I could take. I called some more shelters. Most did not answer their phones at night. I didn't know what else I could do that night. Just wait.

The phone rang again. It was Dorinda's mom and dad. They were calling, hoping like us that there was good news. There wasn't. They told Dorinda to tell me that they were praying and that they had contacted people all over the country to pray. They called it a prayer chain. I had never heard of it before, but I was thankful for all the help I could get. As the dusk turned into night, we continued to get calls from family and friends hoping for good news. Always the same; nothing to report. One-by-one we started to close our eyes and go to sleep. Another evening gone with no results, no clues, no David.

DAY FIVE

Tuesday

When I opened my eyes, sunlight was streaming into our bedroom window. Normally, that would be a welcomed sight. But this seemed like another day ahead full of worry that would end just like the last four—empty. I would be going back to Eastern Michigan to talk to David's other teachers and classes this morning. I didn't feel very enthusiastic about it at all. Still I had to go because I had to try and cover every base, follow every instinct, do everything I could think to do. After taking Tawnie outside for a while, I came back inside to take a shower and get dressed for the trip to the college.

Before leaving, I walked into David's room. Ashley had been sleeping in David's bed but was now gone. She probably went home sometime during the night. I lay down on David's bed and looked up at the ceiling like he must have done thousands of times. I wondered what he was thinking the last time he lay here just like I was doing now. Dorinda looked into the room at me. She stood there briefly, and then she came and lay down next to me. Together we lay there without saying a word. After a while, I told her I must get up and go to Eastern. Getting up slowly, I seemed to feel a lot older today. I guess everything was beginning to take a toll on my body.

Tawnie was lying at the end of the bed, and I nearly stepped on her. Normally the center of attention, she had really been the forgotten one these last few days. I bent down to her and gave her a good massage all over her body. Her white hair was flying everywhere. She was stretching, moaning, and groaning like crazy. Dorinda and I both had a good laugh about her. I left them both and went to the car to drive back to the college.

Once there, I walked straight to David's class. This class and the next went the same as those the day before. A few students asked if they could help in any way. I told them that they could, and I gave them flyers and asked them to pin them up somewhere on campus.

After leaving the last class, I went to the intramural building. This multipurpose building was where David worked with his campus job. After explaining to the young girl at the check-in counter why I was there, she sent me through to talk to the director of the building. He was David's boss. He invited me into his office and told me that he had heard about David's disappearance. He asked me to sit down and explain what had happened. After I went through the story, he told me he couldn't believe it. He said that he thought David was doing well there and that he himself never had a clue. I told him that this was how everyone felt. I asked him if it was okay if I put up flyers around the building, and he said that it was. I thanked him and left.

While putting up a flyer outside of the handball courts, I saw my friend, John. At the same moment, John saw me and came out of the court. John's son Nick had been friends with David for many years. John asked if there was anything he could do to help. I told him that if I thought of anything I would call him. He said that he could not believe it and that he was really sorry. I put up a few more flyers, walked back to the car, and drove home.

On the way home, I thought about David's old high school, Willow Run. I knew that they had a police officer, but I could not recall his name. When I returned home, I went directly to the phone book and looked up the number for the high school. I called the number, and there was no answer. I called again. No answer. What was going on? I was getting extremely frustrated. Dorinda calmed me down. She called the number and someone answered. She asked them the name of the police officer and asked if he was in. His name was Detective Boivin. She wanted to know why we needed to talk to him. Dorinda explained that our son, David, who had just graduated last June, was missing. She said she would leave a message with Detective Boivin to have him call us back. After about ten minutes, the phone rang and it was Detective Boivin. I explained to him what had happened. He asked a lot of questions and took notes. Detective Boivin told me that he worked with the Washtenaw County Sheriffs Department, where I had filed the missing persons report. He said that, even though I had contacted all of these other police agencies, he was really glad that I called him. He wanted to do everything he could to help. He told me that he would be in touch. I thanked him and we hung up.

The phone rang again. It was Dorinda's cousin, Denise Puckett. Denise and her husband Troy pastor a church in Alabama. She wanted to see if there was any news about David. Dorinda told her no, and Denise said they would continue to pray.

Shortly after they hung up, the phone rang again. It was the state police cyber crime unit calling. They wanted to come over in an hour and take a look at our computer to attempt to track whomever David had been talking with. We told them to come over as soon as they could. They said that they had to finish up where they were and then they would be right over. Dorinda had continued watching the computer and had still not learned anything new. She had been making contact with some of David's friends. For the most part, they were just asking her if she had heard anything new. It was about noon.

I had my appointment with the psychic at 4:30. While Dorinda was on the computer, I decided to call shelters in Atlanta again. One after another, I began the routine that I had already been through so many times. As I glanced toward the front window of the house, I noticed a State Police car slowly driving by. As I walked to the front door, I saw that he was pulling into the driveway. When he came to the door, we welcomed him in. He told us his name was Louis Jones. He said he would examine our hard drive to gather any information that he could about those with whom David had been communicating on the Internet. We offered him something to drink, but he said that he didn't need anything and that he wanted to get right to work. I watched him for a while and decided to go back to working the phone. From the kitchen table where I was calling, I occasionally looked in to see the officer working intensely. After a few hours, the officer told us that so far he had found nothing unusual. He had seen no contacts with anyone in or near Atlanta, Dayton, or anywhere else. There was nothing that seemed suspicious. He said that he was not yet finished looking into the computer hard drive but that he had another important appointment and had to leave us for now. He told us he would return again the next day if possible. We thanked him and saw him to the door. Again we had come up with nothing.

The situation seemed to be getting more and more desperate. My hopes dashed again, I sat down on the couch feeling hopeless. My heart was broken; my mind was confused. I felt like I was reaching the end of my rope. As I pulled myself up to go for a paper towel to dry my tears, I looked at the clock in the kitchen. It was 3:30, almost time to leave to go to my appointment with the psychic. I glanced back at the table and saw the list of shelters. Something inside told me that I needed to make one more call before I left. I sat down and looked at the list. The next number on the list was for the Atlanta Church of God. That seemed odd to me. My father-in law built the Willow Run Church of God that sits two blocks from our home. I called the number for the Atlanta church. A woman answered the phone and said that her name was Page. With a very cheerful voice, she asked if she could help me. I told her that I hoped that she could, and I began to tell her the story of David's disappearance. I felt the need to go deeper into the story this time. I told her how I first found the letter and rushed to the Ann Arbor bus station. I told her about Dayton, Lexington, Atlanta, and back to Ypsilanti. Breaking down in tears at times, I continued to tell her about all the police agencies involved and the trips to Eastern Michigan to talk to David's classes. I told her how desperate I was and how lost I felt. My emotions were overwhelming me, and I felt like I was about to fall apart. I could hear her quietly crying on the other end of the phone. She finally spoke these words to me: "Sir, I don't know you, but if you come back to Atlanta looking for David you come straight to this church. You can stay here with us, we will feed you, we will give you a car, we will put someone in the car with you who knows the streets of Atlanta, and if your son is here we will find him." Tears were now flowing down my face. I felt like I had hit rock bottom. Yet this Christian woman's love and compassion had done something to me deep down inside.

As I thanked her and hung up the phone, I looked down at the table. There in the center of the table, lay the Bible. I reached over and picked it up. Sobbing and broken, I held the Bible up in the air looking straight up to God in heaven and said these words: "God, I want to be just like this lady, I want to always be part of the solution, never part of the problem again. If you will save my son, I will serve you for the rest of my life. I will never leave you; I will always be part of the solution, never part of the problem again." As soon as I set the Bible down on the table, the phone rang. David was home. His friend Ross in Ann Arbor was on the phone and told me that David had just gotten off the bus in Ann Arbor and had come to his apartment. David was in the bathroom and didn't know Ross was calling. I dropped the phone and started shouting, dancing, jumping, running, and rejoicing. I pulled out the pack of cigarettes from my pocket, tore them up, and threw them in the trash. I fell down on my knees and started thanking God, praising God, worshipping Him. Dorinda was crying and thanking God. I kept saying over and over, "I'm yours, God; I'm all yours."

After a while I jumped up and grabbed my truck keys and started to run out the door to go and pick David up. As I got to the door, something stopped me. I turned around and told Dorinda that we would wait. David had come this far; we would let him come the rest of the way. It was such a hard decision. But we felt we had to let David come all the way home by himself. The wait was excruciating. We called a few close friends and family and, of course, Ashley. We had been waiting for about an hour when a Washtenaw County Sheriff's patrol car pulled up into our driveway. As I stood in the doorway, I could see David in the car talking with the officer in the car. After a few minutes, David finally stepped out of the car. I ran down the steps and met David coming to the porch. I wrapped my arms around him and held him for a long time. He looked sad, tired, and dirty. I finally let him go and then it was Dorinda's turn. As she hugged David, I walked over to the officer to thank him. I then noticed his nametag. It was Detective Boivin, the Willow Run High School officer, with whom I had talked that morning. He told me that he was driving home from work and saw David walking on the other side of the street. He turned around and pulled up next to David and told him to get in. David resisted at first but Officer Boivin insisted, and David finally got in. He told David how I had called him that morning and how he had said he would do anything that he could to help us. With tears welling up in his eyes, Officer Boivin said that he usually took a different route home but that God had put him in the right place to find David. I told him that I knew that was true. I thanked him again, gave him a hug, and went into the house where David and Dorinda had gone.

David had already gone to take a shower. Dorinda was making food for him to eat, for our son who once was lost now was found. Dorinda and I held each other and gave a huge sigh of relief. The tears now flowing were tears of joy not pain. Not only had my son come home, but also I had received an answer to prayer from God that had completely transformed my very being. Old things had passed away and all things had become new. I fully believe that a portal to heaven had opened up in the sky above that kitchen table and the power of God had transformed me for eternity. I had been delivered at that moment from smoking, drinking, lusting, anger, and many other things. God gave me a new heart. I had been born again.

Even though Dorinda and I were on top of the world, David was not feeling the same way. He had come home, but he was still facing what he

felt like was his failure. I went down into the base-
ment where David had gone to take a shower. He
was now dressed and sitting quietly on the couch.
I asked him if he wanted to talk. He said that he
didn't want to talk. He was hungry and tired. He
said that he just wanted to eat and go to bed. I
told him that I understood. I gave him another
hug and left him alone to think. I went upstairs
and Dorinda and I began to call everyone to let
them know David was home. We began by calling all of our family and friends, followed by the
police agencies and then the shelters. I called the
Dayton Greyhound bus station and talked with
the older man who was there the day I came in.
He promised to tell Calvin, the young man who
had helped me find out that David's bus ticket
had taken him to Atlanta. I insisted on him giving
me his home phone number, so that I could call
him myself. When I called his house, he was very
happy that I had called him with this good news.

David ate his dinner downstairs that night.
It would take a few weeks before he would begin
to open up with us and tell us what he had been
through. David had run away because he had gotten behind in his class work. He could see that he

could not catch up. He felt like he would not be able to make me understand, so he ran. He had gone as far away as his money would take him, thus Atlanta. When he got off the bus in Atlanta, he had twenty dollars. He spent the first night in the YMCA, which had an all- night gymnasium. He rented a locker, bought a little food, and was nearly broke. The next day, he was homeless and broke on the streets. He bumped into one of the homeless men to whom I had given money. He had asked David if his dad drove a red Blazer. David was amazed and said yes, his dad drove a red Blazer. He asked how the homeless man knew that. He told David that his dad was giving out money to anyone on the streets in Atlanta, trying to find him. David realized in his heart that he could go home. He began trying to sell his possessions on the streets to raise money for a bus ticket home. He was scammed and robbed of nearly everything he had with him. Eventually, he made friends with three teenagers who had a sign and were begging for money to get home. They would end up giving David the sign to use. He then took their advice and walked to the airport to beg for money to get home. He eventually got enough money and began his journey back to the bus station. On his way back, at about 2:00 in the morning, he was walking through a dark neighborhood. A car stopped next to him. An older black man asked him what the heck he was doing walking through this neighborhood. David said he was trying to get back to the bus station. The man said that people in this neighborhood would kill a white boy walking through there at night. He ordered David into his car and drove him to the bus station. David said that the man was his guardian angel. I believe he was exactly that.

We would all sleep very well on this night.

AFTERWORD

The next morning, I woke up and walked into David's room to look in on him. He was sound asleep. What a glorious, wonderful sight! I spent much of this day at Eastern Michigan taking down posters and talking to faculty, giving them the good news. Friends and family came by the house, and we continued to call everyone else we could think of to let them know David was home.

I had decided to go back to work on Friday morning. There were four men at work with whom I had been total enemies for quite some time. It had been so bad between us that I had tried to get them to meet me after work to fight. I had even been trying to find out where they lived, so I could go there and hurt them. But now I could not wait to get to work to ask them to forgive me. I did not know what the Bible said about forgiveness. I did not know how Jesus asked God the Father to forgive those who had beat and crucified him. I would learn of this later. But something had changed inside me. God had changed me. I had been born again. I knew that I had to get to those four men and apologize. Even though all along I felt that everything was their fault, it didn't matter. I wanted to make it right. That first morning back to work was unbelievable. As I waited and found them one by one, I told them how sorry I was. I asked them each to please forgive me. I said that I would never be part of the problem again. With amazement, tears, and hugs, all four, one at a time, said that they were also sorry and asked me to forgive them. I, of course, said that I would.

My life was so different now, so much more positive. Thank God! When Dorinda came home from work, I told her what had happened. She could not believe it. I told her that I couldn't wait to get to church on Sunday to thank God for what he had done. That Sunday morning I was so excited to go to church, I could hardly contain myself. The Willow Run Church of God, now known as Victorious Life Church of God, was two blocks away. My father-in-law, G.J. Chandler, had built the church in the early seventies. On this Sunday,

Pastor Ron Stewart was delivering the sermon. He would tell me later that he knew that I would be coming to the altar when he finished. He could see it in my face the whole service. He just didn't know how fast I would be coming. When he finished his sermon and made an altar call, I took off running. I would spend the next thirty minutes on my face crying and thanking God for what he had done, for not only answering my prayer to save my son, but also for completely transforming my heart and my life.

As the weeks went by, we began to get our lives back to normal. Christmas took on a new meaning for us. We had a realization of the important things in life and in Christmas. Dorinda rededicated her life the Sunday after I did. She had been saved at a young age, but had drifted away because of many years of neglecting the things of God. The first few Sundays when the offering was received, I was so thankful that I was giving all the money in my wallet. Dorinda reminded me that we also needed to eat. I agreed, and we made a commitment to start giving ten percent of our income as soon as we could. Several weeks later, we began tithing our ten percent. The next week,

Dorinda received that exact amount in a raise at work. Praise God!

We soon became regulars at every church service. David, though, had yet to come with us. We were asking him to come but not pressuring him. We wanted him to feel what we felt—the presence of God in our lives. David had returned to Eastern Michigan for the winter term with a lighter load of classes. Everything seemed to be working out well.

Easter was approaching, and the church was having an Easter play. We were hoping that David would come to the play. I had been asked to serve as an usher. The day of the Easter play arrived, and David said he would come with us. The play was in the evening, and that afternoon I began feeling sick to my stomach. I told Dorinda that I didn't believe that I could go. Dorinda was more knowledgeable about the Bible than I was. She told me that the devil was behind me feeling sick. She said that he knew that if I didn't go to the play, then David wouldn't go. I prayed and asked God to help me. The sickness went away.

That night David, Dorinda, and I attended the Easter play. Pastor Stewart's son, Justin Stewart, the youth pastor, made a passionate altar call.

David came forward and gave his heart to Jesus. The Lord had done exceedingly, abundantly, more than I had asked.

At my kitchen table weeks before, I had made a vow to God. If he would save my son, I would serve him the rest of my life. He not only saved my son, but he also saved me and Dorinda; and David is now going into ministry. Dorinda is in the choir and the ladies' dance team. I am my pastor's assistant, church chaplain, and work in our church food ministries helping the needy. David is living in Florida, serving in a ministry called Mission Florida through the Abundant Life Church of God in Lakeland, Florida. God is truly amazing. We have seen many miracles of divine healing in our lives since our journey with Christ began. Yet the greatest miracle is the miracle of salvation that Christ gave to all three of us as we were all born again. My love for my son, David, is very great. But the Father's love for us is the greatest love imaginable.

When looking back on the events of those five days, there are a number of things that stand out. My in-laws, G.J. and Carla Chandler, had been praying for us to come to God for many, many years. But also they had been trying to do it themselves. They would call us nearly every weekend to ask if we were either going to church or if we had been to church on Sunday. A week before David disappeared they had made a new decision. They would never again ask a thing about church. They would pray and put it in God's hands. They stopped trusting themselves and started trusting God to do the work. In less then two weeks Dorinda and I had been born again and were fully dedicated to serving God.

Also, I can look back and see how God used and answered the prayers of his children. There were numerous churches praying. There were prayer chains. There was the man that prayed with me in the restaurant. There were so many others who were praying for us. On Monday night of the fourth day of my ordeal, the Willow Run Church of God had a scheduled board meeting. My cousin, Jeff Miller, was a member of that board. Pastor Ron Stewart had presided over my father's funeral but did not know me very well. Earlier on Monday, Pastor Stewart had felt God leading him to pray for me. At the board meeting, Pastor Stewart shared this feeling with my cousin Jeff. Jeff had incredibly felt the same prompting of the Holy Spirit. Neither one knew a thing about David's disappearance. They joined hands and prayed for me that night. God heard and answered the prayers of his people.

I think of Page, the woman with whom I talked in the Atlanta Church of God. Her desire to help me showed me such a true heart for God—something not seen often enough. Her faithfulness to God in tending to the needs of the lost and broken will forever be etched in to my mind.

The greatest miracle of all is how God gave us the heart of Jesus when we were born again. Old things passed away and all things became new. I saw people differently, that we were all children of God and he loved us all equally.

For over five years now, I have worked in our food ministries that serve the needy and senior citizens. I love to go to the hospitals and pray for people, for I know our God works miracles. It is an experiential faith. I know my God is the healer. David also knows God is the healer.

Not long after David received Christ as his savior, he became close friends with our youth pastors, Justin and Jaime Stewart. Both David and Justin are very sports-minded young men. They soon formed a flag football team, which played in an indoor league. I became the cameraman who recorded their games. One night early in a game, David was running hard covering a receiver on defense. As the ball was coming down, David jumped in the air to try to intercept the pass. The receiver's feet bumped David in the air knocking him off balance. David came down on his back, flipped over and ended up on his hands and knees. Justin immediately ran up to him to see if he was okay. He then prayed over him. David slowly got up and walked back to the huddle. He played the rest of the game.

When the game ended, David came up to me and I noticed that his voice sounded different. I asked him if he felt sick. He said that he didn't. The team was going to Justin's house to watch the film from the game. I told David that if he started to feel worse to call me. At 1:00 a.m. David called. He said he felt okay but that Justin said he sounded worse. He was going to go to the emergency room. I jumped out of bed, dressed, and met them there. David seemed to be fine except for the sound of his voice. He sounded like he had a cold.

We waited three hours before being taken back to see a doctor. After examining David, the doctor started acting nervous. He went outside the room and soon the nurses came back with a crash cart, the kind used to restart someone's heart. Dorinda walked in, followed by the doctor. The doctor said that he was ordering x-rays. Soon the x-rays were done and the doctor came in with the news. He said that David had a hole in his esophagus and that he also had a broken neck. He had called the hospital throat specialist. They planned to put a tube down David's throat to find the hole in his esophagus. They would then do immediate surgery.

I was shocked. I told David that I needed to go outside and call people to pray. When Dorinda and I reached the parking lot I remembered something that I had told others when they needed

God: "When you need God get on your face and tell him you need him." Right there in the middle of the road I fell on my hands and knees and cried out to God to heal my son.

After a few minutes we made a few calls and went back inside. The doctor had come to place the tube down David's throat to find the hole. He looked very concerned as he began the procedure. After a few minutes he began to look puzzled. Then he looked at me and smiled. As he started shaking his head side to side he said that it didn't make any sense. There was air behind David's lungs. The only way for it to get there was for there to be a hole in his esophagus. But there was no hole or at least there wasn't one now. Just then another doctor came in with a second set of x-rays of David's neck. The break that they saw in the first set of x-rays was gone. God had healed David.

The specialist soon came into our room. She said that they were admitting him into surgical intensive care. She would later tell me that when the emergency room had called her, the first question that she asked them was, "Is the patient still alive?" She told us that with this injury, if there is not surgery within one hour, one hundred percent of the patients die. Of those who received surgery within the hour ninety percent still die. David never had any surgery at all. God again had shown His miraculous power by answering prayer and healing David.

After several days, the doctors finally decided to discharge David. Four doctors, including the specialist, came into his room. They told us that they knew that we were Christians, so they could give us their opinion. They said that they had no explanation for what had happened to David except that God had healed him. Praise my God!

There have been other miraculous healings in our lives. My back pain was healed as I sang in the choir one day. Also my leg was healed after two weeks of pain. Another miraculous time when God showed me his power was when I was going through a time of hurt. I had gone with our church youth group as a chaperone to a youth event called Winterfest in Knoxville, Tennessee. I had heard about the previous trips the youth had taken to Winterfest. I had heard how Spirit-filled the trips had been. I had also witnessed for myself the on-fire-for-God spirit the youth had shown when they had returned from previous Winterfest events. I was so excited to be a part of this trip, but the trip did not turn out like I was expecting.

We had problems with our bus driver, problems with our hotel, and even our kids seemed to be uninterested in worshipping God. I wound up very discouraged. On the trip home I was in the front seat behind the driver. I had been riding with my head down and my eyes closed for hours. I had been crying and really complaining to God. I finally started telling God that I was going to leave my church and go somewhere else. As clear as I have ever heard God speak, he said, "Don't forget what I did for you." I jerked my head up and my eyes were looking out the right side windows of the bus. There, across the street from our bus, was the Dayton, Ohio bus station where I had first looked for David. In shock I asked the bus driver where we were. He said we were in downtown Dayton. I asked him why? He said there had been an accident on the highway and they had detoured traffic around the accident. In a time of discouragement when I was telling God that I was going to walk away from the church where he had placed me in to serve, God had reminded me how he had answered my prayers.

God's timing is perfect. He truly is an on-time God. God has given me other important dreams as he also has given them to David. It has been truly amazing and miraculous what God has done in all three of our lives. Dorinda has been given a heart of compassion that reaches out to those that are suffering through sickness, or heartache. God gives to David revelation, knowledge, and enlightenment for ministry drama and messages to the church and the lost. The Lord has given me a heart to worship Him and a strong faith to believe in the power of God for healing and any type of miracle. My God can do *anything!*

FROM DAVID

As you've no doubt already noticed, God had His sovereign fingerprint intricately woven into my father's story, but the story didn't stop there. For my life, the story was just beginning.

After being saved during an Easter service in 2003, I spent the next few years bouncing around colleges trying to figure out just how God fit into my future plans. I found myself drawn to the spiritual calling He placed on my life but didn't know how to equate that into real world living. In the midst of this time of searching, I came into contact with a group called Master's Commission at a few different youth conferences and was blown away at their drama ministry. As impacted as I was by their drama performances, I never dreamed I would ever join that group or even another like it. Little did I know that God had other plans for my life.

In 2006, the youth pastors' ministry I grew under for three years began to become extremely interested in starting a version of Master's Commission through the Church of God entitled The Mission. By the first month of 2007, my youth pastor, his wife, and myself were all certified leaders within the denomination for the Mission program and had plans to start in the fall. We started with nine students that year and have been watching God change the hearts and lives of every person that has passed through our program. We recently celebrated the graduation of our third year on May 23rd, 2010.

In the span of my time in the Mission program, I've had the privilege to minister through house leading, preaching, teaching, media, graphics, web building, drama, evangelism, and countless opportunities for servanthood. The environments God has allowed me to minister in are as varied as the people I've ministered to: carnivals, beautiful Catholic sanctuaries, enormous arenas, public elementary, middle schools, high schools, well-known Christian universities, and even a small, sweaty Bahamian church in everywhere from big cities to middle-of-nowhere towns. Some of the highlights of those opportunities include spending five days documenting a clothing drop in earthquake ravaged Haiti, ministering in drama to over 25,000 on two separate occasions and carrying a 60 pound cross witnessing with a fellow Mission student 100 miles down the coast of Florida during spring break.

I could take page upon page to share the goodness of God that's been shed upon my life, but I feel more impressed to leave you with two scriptures to help encourage and strengthen you in your walk with the Lord. The first, as cliché as it has become at times, is Jeremiah 29:11 which simply says, "For I know the plans I have for you," says the LORD. "They are plans for good and not for disaster, to give you a future and a hope." (NLT) My life seemed as though it was headed for nothing but disaster with no chance of a future or a hope but the Lord had other plans, and He does for you too.

The last scripture I want to leave with you can be found in 1 Corinthians 1:27, and it reads, "Instead, God deliberately chose things the world considers foolish in order to shame those who think they are wise. And he chose those who are powerless to shame those who are powerful." (NLT) God plucked me, a runaway, college-flunking kid who was lost in Atlanta, out of a dead-end life, then radically changed my life and placed me in a position to minister all across the world. That's foolish to the world's eyes and even my own at times, to be honest. You may feel like it would be foolish for God to use you in such a way too; however, be encouraged at the fact that God doesn't look on the outside. He looks at the heart (1 Samuel 16:7). Let your heart be changed by the father's love and be amazed as you experience the future He has planned for you.

NUMBERS 30:2

If a man vow a vow unto the Lord, or swear an oath to bind his soul with a bond; he shall not break his word, he shall do according to all that proceedeth out of his mouth.

PSALM 65:1

Praise waiteth for thee, O God, in Zion: and unto thee shall the vow be performed.

I WILL SERVE YOU FOREVER LORD!

BACK ROW: Adam, David, Shane
FRONT ROW: Dorinda and Dave